Justinian I

A Captivating Guide to Justinian the Great and How This Emperor Ruled the Roman Empire

Free Bonus from Captivating History (Available for a Limited time)

Hi History Lovers!

Now you have a chance to join our exclusive history list so you can get your first history ebook for free as well as discounts and a potential to get more history books for free! Simply visit the link below to join.

Captivatinghistory.com/ebook

Also, make sure to follow us on Facebook, Twitter and Youtube by searching for Captivating History.

Contents

Introduction

While the name Justinian may not be one that instantly strikes a chord with people, his life and his legacy continue to impact people all over the world to this day. It is very likely that as you read this, you are living your life in accordance with laws that came about as a result of Justinian's rewriting of the old Roman codes. Your religious life may have been impacted by the religious melting pot of the Byzantine Empire, and you may not even realize it. Perhaps even some of the characters in the books you read, the movies you watch, and the games you play are actually taken from the lives of real people who lived in a very different world than ours, and yet they have captured the imaginations of creative thinkers throughout the centuries.

We know about the life of Justinian from various sources, and as with all historical accounts, it is important to remember that a lot of history was written with an agenda in mind. This is very true when it comes to looking at the life of Justinian I. The famous Byzantine Greek historian Procopius is a major source for modern historians on Justinian. While Procopius began by praising Emperor Justinian I and enshrining his many accomplishments, he later villainizes both Justinian and his wife with lots of damning indictments of their wickedness. It is worth bearing in mind that we cannot necessarily trust either the glowing reports written under the emperor's patronage or the outrageous gossip written once that patronage was taken away. The truth undoubtedly lies somewhere in the middle ground, and it is up to historians to try to establish the truth.

What we can be much surer of are the political achievements of Justinian, his important legal work, and the incredible record of the extraordinary buildings that were erected in his name. The artistic offerings of the Byzantine Empire under his reign have produced artifacts that can attest to the flourishing cultural atmosphere of the time.

However, perhaps the most interesting aspects of Justinian's life are those for which we must try to fill in the blanks: his humble origins, his rise to power, and his legendary relationship with one of history's most intriguing women, Theodora.

Chapter 1 – Early Life

The ruler who came to be known as Justinian was born in 482 under the name Flavius Petrus Sabbatius Justianus to a peasant woman named Vigilantia. There is very little source material to tell us about his early life—probably owing to the fact that he was of low birth—so to give us an idea of what life may have been like for the young Justinian, let's take a look at the world he was born into.

Justinian was born in Tauresium, in the Roman province of Dardania. At this time, the Roman Empire had become fractured and weakened. The Western Roman Empire had fallen, and the Eastern Roman Empire was under threat on all sides. The Eastern Roman Empire would remain the last remnant of the Roman Empire until its eventual fall in 1453; it would be in 1557 that the name Byzantine Empire came about, which is how it is often referred to today. Life was fairly turbulent for those near the borders of the empire, as they were under threat of invasion, and even those who were relatively safe from violence had the threat of political and economic instability.

We know very little of the child's father, Sabbatius, or his profession. It is likely that he was a farmer, as his mother's family had been. However, it was Justinian's adoptive father—his uncle, Justin—who would change the fortunes of the young Justinian and, in doing so, change the world.

Adoption by Justin

Justin may have begun life as a lowly farmer, but he left his rural home as a young man and went to Constantinople in search of a better life. He joined the army and fought in a number of battles, rising through the ranks to become the commander of the imperial guard, known as the Excubitors. These guards were top-ranking soldiers who had proven their loyalty and skills in order to be granted the honor of protecting the ruler, who at that time was Emperor Anastasius I.

Finding himself in a position of relative power and influence, Justin took his nephew under his wing, adopting him (which is when he took on the name Justinian) and taking him to Constantinople to be educated. As a result, Justinian received an education that Justin himself could only have dreamed of. He was taught history, theology, and the theory of law. It is likely he would have gained important skills such as oration as well. Some historical sources suggest that Justinian himself also served as a member of the Excubitors.

Justinian developed a strong sense of loyalty to Justin, his adoptive father, who essentially set him free from the life of a peasant by giving him an education and an introduction to proper society. In return, Justinian supported Justin in his claim to power. Against all the odds, Justin was poised to take the place of the ruler who he was employed to protect. He had served as a senator, and in 518, the death of Emperor Anastasius, who left no clear heir, gave way to a power vacuum that a number of powerful men sought to fill.

Justin's Rise to Power

The Senate held a meeting to debate on who should become the next ruler of the Byzantine Empire. Time was of the essence; the Senate wanted to be in control of the decision in order to secure their own hold on power, and yet there was much unrest among the potential candidates. It was important to avoid conflict or risk destabilizing the government, especially when the threat of invasion from neighboring territories left the weakened empire feeling insecure. After much debate, Justin was chosen as the successor of Anastasius in 518. However, this did not mean that he could relax. Many others were unhappy about the choice, most notably the nephews of Anastasius, who felt they had more of a right to rule.

It was urgent that Justin legitimize his claim to power and reassure the Senate and the people that he was the right person for the role. Securing his power was made possible by Justinian, who proved to be increasingly intelligent when it came to planning and resourceful when it came to making things happen. Justin was illiterate, spoke Latin as opposed to Greek, and had little in the way of education. He was a self-made success, but this left him vulnerable to criticism and distrust, and so, he relied heavily upon experienced advisors. Justinian was his most important advisor and became an integral part of Justin's reign.

With Justin I in power, Justinian removed the threat of those who opposed him, mainly by executing and exiling his rivals. He also secured the loyalty of prisoners in return for their freedom and ensured that Justin's reign was protected by efficient military forces. Justin I's rule brought one major change to the Byzantine Empire— he was an Orthodox Christian, while previous rulers had been Monophysites. The major difference in the two beliefs related to how they each perceived the nature of Jesus Christ; the conflict arose over the dual nature of Christ as both divine and human. These differences in doctrine had led to huge religious and political disagreements between different parts of what had been the Roman Empire. By bridging the gap between the Roman Catholic Church and that of the Byzantine Church, and forging stronger links back to Rome, Justinian helped Justin to implement major religious changes in the empire.

Without Justinian, it is doubtful whether Justin could have held onto his power. However, Justinian proved to be a loyal and effective supporter, and many writers of the time and since have attributed much of the real power to Justinian rather than his uncle. Justinian was certainly becoming more influential and powerful as time went on. His passionate interest in restoring the Eastern Roman Empire to how it had been in its glory days was only growing. As a keen politician, he was a regular attendee at the most important social and political events of the day, which were—surprisingly—the chariot races.

Chariot Races

Imagine all of the passion that modern societies have for team sports like football and soccer. Then imagine that there are just two teams, the Greens and the Blues. Now imagine that not only are those two teams rivals when it comes to racing, but they are also politically and religiously opposed to one another. Now imagine enormous stadiums, known as hippodromes, where up to one hundred thousand people can meet to watch the races and cheer on their team. Even women, who were so often excluded from other sports, were allowed to be spectators. The importance of the chariot races in the Byzantine Empire can really not be understated! The races were dangerous, thrilling, and so much more than just sport. People stuck with absolute loyalty to their team, with races often erupting into violence. Justinian was a keen supporter of the Blues, and it was here that he met another Blues fan who would change his life forever.

Her name was Theodora, and together they would go on to become one of the most powerful reigning couples the world has ever seen.

Chapter 2 – Empress Theodora

Theodora was born around the year 500. While sources vary about the details of her background, it is generally believed that she was of Greek Cypriot heritage and probably born in Cyprus. Her father was employed as a trainer of bears, providing thrilling entertainment for the people attending the famous Hippodrome of Constantinople—the same place where the chariot races took place—but he died when Theodora was very young. Her mother was an actress and performer, so when she found herself widowed with young children, she was forced to remarry immediately to secure the family's future. It is recorded that after her husband died and she had remarried, she presented her young girls to the Green faction and their thousands of supporting fans. The poverty-stricken children were directed to charm the audience, begging for their new stepfather to be given their father's old job with the Greens. When they were met with ridicule and taunting, the Blue faction seized the opportunity to gain some kudos with the public and charitably offered Theodora's mother's new husband a job. This was a rare case of switching loyalties from one faction to the other, but it would come to have an extremely profound effect on the life of Theodora.

Life as a Performer

Theodora was reportedly very beautiful and elegant. With few options for making a living, Theodora and her sisters became performers while they were still children. Often described as an actress, the word has connotations of prostitution, and it is widely assumed that Theodora was first a child prostitute and then an actress. This would have meant performing sexual acts on stage as well as privately. She may have been engaged in performances of stripping, acrobatics, dancing, and play-acting, and she was most well known for her performance of the story of Leda and the Swan, which was performed using geese. It was a lewd industry, and women were heavily exploited. The threat of poverty and violence was very real, and succeeding as an actress and prostitute was, at times, the only option for young women such as Theodora.

Religious Conversion

As a teenager, Theodora made a rather unconventional choice and left her position to travel with an official who was journeying to Libya. She lived with him as his mistress for three or four years before traveling to Egypt, where she had a religious conversion and became a firm believer in Miaphysite Christianity. This is the belief that the dual nature of Christ—both mortal and divine—is actually one inseparable nature. This contrasts with the beliefs of Emperor Justin I and Theodora's future husband, Justinian. However, when Theodora left Egypt and spent time in the company of a friend named Macedonia, who is believed to have been a dancer who was also employed as a spy, which would have been a common occupation during this time of political and religious uncertainty.

Theodora and Justinian

The story of how a prostitute of low birth became one of the most powerful women ever to have lived is one that captures the imagination of many people, and yet we do not know exactly how she met Justinian or what their life together was like before they were married. We know that she returned to Constantinople around the age of 21, and it must have been soon afterward that she met Justinian.

At this point, during the years 518 to 521, Justinian was becoming increasingly important to Emperor Justin. He had been made consul and commander of the army, and despite his lack of experience as a soldier, he was a trusted military commander. Justin is believed to have become gradually unstable and suffered from senility as he grew older. He has been described as a doddering old man in accounts by Procopius. Justinian stepped in and was essentially the real power and authority behind the scenes when Justin was unable to rule effectively

When Justinian and Theodora met, he was around twenty years older than her. This may have raised a few eyebrows, but the real issue was the fact that it was illegal for anyone of the senatorial rank, which Justinian was a part of, to marry an actress. It is thought that they lived together anyway, and Justinian took parental responsibility for Theodora's illegitimate daughter, a child she had when she was just fourteen years old. Justinian raised the child as his own despite her obviously not being his biological child. To legitimize the relationship, Theodora and Justinian had to marry, and it was another woman who stood in the way of this happening: Empress Euphemia. Justinian's aunt by marriage to his uncle Justin, Euphemia had been a slave and a concubine before she was the empress, and so it is perhaps surprising that she was so against Justinian marrying Theodora because of her low birth and immoral occupation. Powerful men often married women of low birth who had won beauty contests, so there was a tradition there that would have made the match a little less shocking to wider society; however, it was still considered a scandal. Euphemia was determined that the marriage would not take place, and it was not until after her death in 523 or 524 that Justin changed the law to permit the marriage and also to legitimize Theodora's daughter. This was reasonable repayment for the many things that Justinian had done for him to secure his power, and the pair married around the year 525.

Empress Theodora

Justin I died on August 1st, 527, and Justinian was naturally his chosen heir. Despite her low birth—or perhaps because of it—Theodora deeply loved the ritual and ceremony of court life. She was crowned as empress alongside her husband when he became emperor the same day Justin died. Remarkably, Justinian insisted that his wife be crowned as his equal; she was to rule alongside him rather than simply being given the title "Empress" because she was his consort. Just two years after their marriage, before which she was considered to be the lowest of the low in society, Theodora was not only married to a powerful man whom she loved, giving her status and respect, but she also found herself Empress of the Eastern Roman Empire.

Her humble beginning in life apparently did not lead to a humble attitude when she was enthroned in power, however! A visit to the court of Theodora was reportedly a terrifying experience for any government official. She required everyone to prostrate themselves, kiss her shoes, and refrain from speaking unless spoken to. Having been little more than a slave to men of higher status, Theodora ensured that as empress, men of status were treated as little more than her slaves. We get a small hint that perhaps she had more understanding of how transitory power is, however, in her most famous quote, "For my own part, I adhere to the maxim of antiquity, that the throne is a glorious sepulcher."

Chapter 3 – Rebellion, Riot, and Rebuilding

Justinian I came to power in the year 527. Despite having already been the de facto ruler for a while under Justin I, not everyone was happy with his succession. His early reign was dogged with problems, and yet he established his aims and set about achieving them with an energy and determination that earned him a reputation as "the emperor who never sleeps."

Justinian's aims were lofty and ambitious; he wanted to restore the Roman Empire to the greatness it once enjoyed and regain control over the Western Roman Empire. Part of this was his plan to unify the Christian church and bring in sweeping law reforms. These law reforms were one of his most urgent and immediate priorities when he came to power, and they would go on to be his most lasting legacy, extending their reach into the fabric of modern-day society.

Justinian assembled a team, headed up by Tribonian, who was the highest legal expert in the Byzantine Empire, to completely revise and redraft the entire Roman code of law. This was a mammoth task, one which would take five years to complete. Just as his predecessor Justin I had done, Justinian judiciously surrounded himself with talented advisors who could offer real expertise. By employing military men with experience, he could have confidence in his armies. By employing finance ministers who understood the economy and his plans for the empire, Justinian was able to collect taxes more efficiently, increasing his funds and allowing him to implement the reforms he wanted and equip the army as he needed.

Unfortunately, it was this policy of employing talented advisors that contributed to his first major test as the emperor; people were dissatisfied with the way Justinian was choosing to govern, as they distrusted his chosen advisors and were worried about the changes to taxes and the law. This led to civil unrest; while Justinian's trusted experts were engaged in a huge project to rewrite the law, the people on the streets were rejecting the very authority of the emperor himself.

The Nika Riots

While the Nika riots were short-lived, beginning on January 13th, 532, and ending after just five full days, it was one of the bloodiest rebellions ever to occur within the Eastern Roman Empire. The hippodrome and its competing factions were to provide the setting for this dark time. Political and social issues were frequently raised at races, with the emperor coming under immense pressure from the public as demands were made between races regarding policy, the appointment of governors, and reform issues. Sometimes this would spill over into violence, with the competing supporters forming mobs that were an unstoppable force, even with a heavy military presence keeping careful watch. Unless the guards and army posted to keep the peace had the agreement of the leaders of the different color factions, they were powerless to intervene if things got out of hand. Murders were not uncommon, but those guilty of murder at a race were put to death.

This is precisely what should have happened in 532 when violence broke out and a man was killed in the stands of the hippodrome. However, the murderers were able to escape and took refuge in a church. The mob was angry; some were defending the men, protecting them from their rivals, while others were desperately trying to reach the men to kill him. Justinian had to calm the situation; he knew that this violence was symptomatic of a larger sense of dissatisfaction that the people were feeling. Not only did they resent higher levels of taxation, but some of his advisors had also proved unpopular with the people as well.

To diffuse the tension, Justinian announced that a chariot race would be held. Instead of having the murderers put to death, he reduced their sentence to imprisonment. This made neither side happy; the Blues wanted them killed, while the Greens insisted they be freed without punishment. When it came time for the chariot race, the crowd was already worked up, and the atmosphere was tense. Supporters of the Blue and Green factions soon turned on a common enemy—Justinian himself. The riots became known as the Nika riots because the supporters' chants changed from the traditional support for their respective teams to the word "Nika!" which translates as "Conquer!" Had Justinian actually been in the hippodrome, he would undoubtedly have been killed, but as he was in his royal box watching the race from the safety of his palace next door, the crowds attacked the palace and held it under siege. Demands were made, which were supported by some members of the Senate who took this opportunity to try to get rid of Justinian. Among these demands were that the governor in charge of taxes, John the Cappadocian, and Tribonian, who was in charge of the law reform, both be dismissed from service.

The violence soon spread across the city, and it is estimated that half of the city was burned to the ground, including many of the important historic buildings such as the Church of the Holy Wisdom, which became known as the Hagia Sophia, where Justinian had held his coronation. A new emperor was named, Hypatius, the nephew of the former Emperor Anastasius (who you will remember was not happy with the succession of Justin I after the death of his uncle). However, Hypatius would never come to real power, despite having the support of the people.

Under siege, with his city aflame and control seized by competing angry mobs, Justinian began to talk about leaving the city. He made plans to escape by ship and take his advisors and his wife Theodora with him as fugitives. This gave rise to a now-famous speech by Theodora, who refused to give up her role as empress, even if it meant death.

> My lords, the present occasion is too serious to allow me to follow the convention that a woman should not speak in a man's council. Those whose interests are threatened by extreme danger should think only of the wisest course of action, not of conventions.

> In my opinion, flight is not the right course, even if it should bring us to safety. It is impossible for a person, having been born into this world, not to die; but for one who has reigned it is intolerable to be a fugitive. May I never be deprived of this purple robe, and may I never see the day when those who meet me do not call me empress.

> If you wish to save yourself, my lord, there is no difficulty. We are rich; over there is the sea, and yonder are the ships. Yet reflect for a moment whether, when you have once escaped to a place of security, you would not gladly exchange such safety for death. As for me, I agree with the adage that the royal purple is the noblest shroud.

It was altogether too rousing and emotive to resist, and Justinian was completely swayed by her. He agreed to stay in Constantinople and fight to save himself and his city. He sent Narses, a great general and a eunuch, to bribe the leaders of the Blues with gold, pointing out that Justinian was a loyal supporter of the Blues since childhood, whereas the would-be emperor Hypatius was a loyal Green supporter. This actually worked. Hypatius was supposed to have been made emperor that very day, but the Blues walked out of the hippodrome where the coronation was to take place. Instead, Justinian's armies, led by his loyal commanders Mundus and Belisarius, marched in and slaughtered the Greens. Over thirty thousand people lost their lives inside the hippodrome that day, and the Nika riots were over.

Justinian was careful to ensure that no traces of this rebellion were allowed to remain. Encouraged by Theodora, the usurper Hypatius was executed, along with any senators who had lent him their support. Not only did this bloody conclusion to the riots rid Justinian of rebels within the Greens and in his Senate, but it also reaffirmed his authority and served as a stark warning to any dissenting voices that may have considered plotting against him in the future. With the city in ruins, Justinian set about rebuilding with his usual energetic and resilient attitude. He restored the city and built some of the largest and most impressive buildings that Constantinople had ever seen, including the lavish Hagia Sophia, which replaced the earlier Church of the Holy Wisdom on the same site. This helped to restore his reputation in the minds of his citizens. With the rebellion quashed, the city being rebuilt beyond its former glory, and his reputation as a powerful emperor secured, Justinian was able to set about achieving his ambitions as emperor, and none of these were more important at this stage than the law reform that he had been so passionate about implementing.

Chapter 4 – Corpus Juris Civilis

After the Nika riots, Justinian redoubled his efforts on his planned law reforms. It was essential to the success of his reign that the law be firmly reestablished. No one had ever undertaken such a broad rewriting of the Roman legal code before, but Justinian was motivated by the large number of constitutions and the plethora of unnecessary court proceedings that arose from them; many of these legal cases arose simply because the law was unclear or contradictory. There were many inconsistencies, constitutions that had become irrelevant, and contradictory laws, which resulted in much confusion. By systematically working through all of the components of the legal code, the law itself could be simplified, and this would make it easier and more effective to implement. It also would make it easier to impose the law on territories that Justinian planned to conquer.

It was an arduous and difficult project since they were going to reevaluate all the laws. It was not just the criminal justice system that they were overhauling but also laws governing society, such as those dealing with inheritance and marriage. Thousands of documents from a wide range of sources had to be studied, some of which were hundreds of years old. Tribonian had been assigned to lead a group of legal experts and scribes to undertake the project soon after Justinian became emperor, and he was tasked to continue after the Nika riots, despite the fact that his unpopularity had led to the public calling for him to be dismissed from his duties.

One of the main reasons for rewriting the laws in this way was, in fact, to promote peace. In the Code of Justinian, a preface explains this theory:

> "The maintenance of the integrity of the government depends upon two things, namely, the force of arms and the observance of the laws: and, for this reason, the fortunate race of the Romans obtained power and precedence over all other nations in former times, and will do so forever, if God should be propitious; since each of these has ever required the aid of the other, for, as military affairs are rendered secure by the laws, so also are the laws preserved by force of arms."

> — The Second Preface

In the year 534, a final draft of the *Corpus Juris Civilis* ("Body of Civil Law") was completed. It consisted of four distinct sections.

Codex Justinianus

Made up of twelve books, the Codex was the first part of the *Corpus Juris Civilis* to be completed. The Codex Justinianus sets out all of the imperial edicts that had been issued since the time of Hadrian in 117. This incorporated the last major legal work that had been created, called the Codex Theodosianus. All of the pronouncements were organized carefully by theme rather than by the ruler who had made them. Justinian added to the codex as he made his own imperial edicts, and a copy of the Codex Justinianus containing his own legislation, dated to 534, still survives.

One of the most important elements of the Codex Justinianus is how it deals with religion. The first of the twelve books was dedicated to matters of religion, and it sets out the status of Christianity as the official religion of the Byzantine Empire. This was essentially Justinian's way of incorporating the church into the state; any citizen of the empire would only remain a citizen if they were a part of the church. The first law insists that all those living within the empire must be Christians, and heresy was not to be tolerated. Pagan practices were also outlawed.

Digest

Also known in Greek as the *Pandectae* ("Encyclopedia"), the Digest is a compilation of legal writings and opinions by legal experts. The idea behind this was that these juristic pieces could be used in court, allowing those involved in a case—and the judges themselves—to refer to the wisdom and experience of various respected and celebrated Roman minds. The Digest was made up of fifty books containing the edited wisdom of great legal minds of the past, organized by topic to make it easier to use. The importance of the Digest was that although legal writings from the past had always been an important part of the legal process, this was the first time that they had actually been given the force of the law. Instead of referring to a snippet from these writings to help inform a case or sway a judge, the Digest was to be considered legally binding.

The Institutiones

Aimed at making the law easier to understand and learn for students of the law, as this would undoubtedly result in a more effective legal system, the *Institutiones Justiniani* ("Institutes of Justinian") was basically a textbook for law students. This consisted of four books, each dealing with one of the four sections of the *Corpus Juris Civilis*.

The Novellae Constitutiones

This section was reserved for new laws (*novellae constitutiones* literally means "new laws"). This allowed the three other parts of the law to stand alone, while new edicts could be incorporated into the *Novellae*. This is particularly useful to historians as it gives insight into how the law changed over time, allowing them to track social change and providing insight into the development of civil rights for oppressed groups such as women, children, and slaves.

The Impact of the Corpus Juris Civilis

The impact of Justinian's new legal code cannot be underestimated. New laws were added, and parts of the *Corpus* were revised, but the fundamental body of work remained throughout the centuries. Not only did it persist for nearly a thousand years until the eventual collapse of the Byzantine Empire, but it also went on to form the basis for much of the Western legal system. The laws that govern many Western countries to this day have evolved from the *Corpus Juris Civilis* that Justinian produced. Translated from the original Latin into Greek, it became the basis for legal training all over Europe, influencing lawmakers throughout history.

Theodora and the Law

While Justinian revolutionized the way people understood the law, changing the legal landscape of the world forever, Empress Theodora was also challenging the status quo and implementing real and lasting social change that then made its way into law. Justinian had once referred to Theodora as the "partner in my deliberations," meaning the issues that mattered to Theodora mattered to Justinian.

Theodora took particular interest in increasing the rights of women in society. Her past as a prostitute gave her a passion for protecting women who were forced into the sex trade. Theodora ensured that forced prostitution was outlawed and wrote a treatise making it illegal for anyone to act as a pimp. Brothels were closed down, and women who had been forced into prostitution were often provided for rather than being left to fend for themselves. There are even accounts of Theodora buying women who were for sale (women could be sold for as little as the price of a pair of sandals) and then freeing them. A convent was also set up for women who had escaped prostitution to live safely.

It was not only the issue of prostitution that Theodora was passionate about; she also implemented sweeping reforms to the rights of women when it came to owning property, marriage, and divorce. Women were given new rights of guardianship over their own children, something that had previously been denied them. Theodora also introduced anti-rape laws in which rape was punishable by death, and she repealed the death sentence for women who committed adultery.

Her incredible achievements as a champion of the rights of women have to be balanced by the reports of her distrust of women of higher status and her forceful habit of "rescuing" women who may not have desired to be rescued. However, it is also worth remembering that all the accounts of Theodora's life and actions were written by men who were likely to have felt, at best, threatened, if not scandalized, by her. There is no doubt that the changes Theodora made completely transformed the lives of many women from the lower rungs of society, and these changes were enshrined in law so that she effectively protected the rights of women well into the future.

Chapter 5 – Expansion of the Empire

With the Nika riots quashed, the great city of Constantinople being rebuilt on a grand scale, and his team of legal experts working on the *Corpus Juris Civilis*, Emperor Justinian I turned his mind back to his ultimate aim: the restoration of the Roman Empire.

Before he could expand his territory and reclaim the land and people that had been lost when the Roman Empire crumbled, he had to first put an end to the war with the Sassanid Empire, a Persian dynasty, which he had inherited from his uncle, Emperor Justin I. Between the years of 527 and 532, Justinian's Roman forces battled the Sassanids for control of the eastern border of the Byzantine Empire. The war saw victories and defeats on both sides, and it only ended after the Persian king, Kavad I, died. This gave Justinian the opportunity to secure a peace deal with the new king, Khosrow I, for which he paid dearly, as it was recorded that it cost eleven thousand pounds of gold. This fee earned him peace and protection on the eastern side so that he could focus on reclaiming territory in the West, toward Rome itself.

War with the Vandals

In the year 533, Justinian's forces invaded the territory of the Vandal Kingdom. The Vandals were a powerful force. They were of Germanic origin, and they had fought against a number of formidable enemies, including the Huns and the Goths. They invaded and settled in North Africa in 429, where they had established a kingdom by 439. The Vandals had plundered Rome in the year 455, yet relations between them and the Eastern Roman Empire had been good until the Vandal king, Hilderic, was deposed. He sought the support of Justinian to defeat the usurper of the throne, Hilderic's cousin Gelimer.

Justinian tasked his best general, Belisarius, with leading a force of fifteen thousand of Justinian's men, along with a barbarian army. The Vandals had forces twice the size of the invading armies, but they were caught off guard in a time of peace when their military lacked training and supplies. As a result, Belisarius was able to forge ahead and defeat the Vandals at the Battle of Ad Decimum on September 13th, 533. The Roman victory was due in part to the poor leadership of King Gelimer, who was distraught at the death of his brother. Soon after the battle, Belisarius captured Carthage, and although he was too late to rescue the deposed King Hilderic, who had been murdered when Gelimer heard that the Roman troops were arriving, he famously devoured a sumptuous meal that had been prepared for the king.

King Gelimer, along with his family and entourage, escaped to Numidia, where they sought refuge in the mountains after the Roman troops took control of Carthage. They were soon under siege by Belisarius' men, and due to the threat of either starving or being attacked, they were forced to surrender in the spring of 534. Gelimer was taken to Constantinople and paraded through the streets, but he was shown mercy and given land in Galatia (modern-day Turkey), where he lived a long life.

The defeat of the Vandals meant Justinian was able to reclaim territory not just in North Africa but also territory in Corsica and Sardinia, as well as the Balearic Islands.

Reclaiming Italy

In 535, Justinian pulled Belisarius out of Africa and sent him to Sicily. As was to be the norm with Justinian's military endeavors, he did not go to battle himself but instead chose talented generals such as Belisarius, who had proven himself in Africa, to lead his campaigns. The political situation in Italy had broken down due to an ongoing power struggle among the Ostrogoths.

The Ostrogoths, the eastern branch of the Goths, had invaded and established the Ostrogothic Kingdom of Italy in 493. In 534, the Ostrogoth King Athalaric died, and by 535, the Ostrogoths had fallen into squabbling among themselves over who would rule. Athalaric's mother, Queen Amalasuntha, had been imprisoned by Theodahad, who had claimed the throne after Athalaric's death. Procopius reports that Justinian and Amalasuntha had a close diplomatic relationship, so Justinian wanted her freed. Her murder, while she was under the "care" of Theodahad's guards, was suspected to be an execution under the orders of Theodahad. This was the opportunity that Justinian needed to enter Italy under the guise of helping to restore the monarchy.

In 535, Belisarius took seven and a half thousand men and began his invasion at Sicily, where he faced little opposition. Emboldened, the armies moved in to attack mainland Italy, capturing Naples first by placing it under siege and then moving on to Rome, after having been invited by the pope. At this point, the Ostrogoths had replaced Theodahad with a new king, King Vitigis. He was not inclined to give up his recently obtained power without a fight and set out to reclaim Rome, placing the city under siege. However, after over a year of being under siege, from 537 until 538, Rome was still under the control of Justinian's forces. Rather than withdrawing, Justinian sent more troops into Italy under General Narses. While this army was successful in taking Milan, it soon fell again to the Ostrogoths, and Narses was pulled out of Italy in 539 due to a conflict between him and Belisarius. Italy was proving more difficult to conquer than had initially seemed.

In 540, Belisarius progressed through Italy toward Ravenna in the north of the country. Ravenna was the capital of the Ostrogothic territory, and so, capturing it would have meant that Belisarius had defeated the Ostrogoths. Instead, they offered Belisarius the opportunity to become an emperor in his own right, the Western Roman emperor. Belisarius accepted the offer of power and entered the city. However, Belisarius had no intention of betraying Justinian, and once he entered the city peacefully under the pretense of becoming the emperor, his men were essentially able to claim the city for Justinian with virtually no opposition. He returned to Constantinople with the now-deposed King Vitigis as a prisoner.

Conflict in the Sassanid Empire

The success in Italy was short-lived, as Justinian was forced to recall Belisarius to deal with new problems with the Sassanid Empire in the early 540s This was partly because of the conflict in the Sassanid Empire, but there is evidence to suggest that Justinian was jealous of Belisarius' popularity and started to become fearful that he may rise up against him. The peace agreement that Justinian had come to with the Persians had been broken by King Khosrow I when he invaded territory belonging to the Eastern Roman Empire. Justinian had little choice but to meet the demands of the king, and he had to sacrifice a lot of gold as tribute in order to protect his empire. Belisarius was able to make some progress against the Persian armies, but they were fairly evenly matched, and they were also hampered by the outbreak of plague. The war with the Sassanid Empire continued until the year 562. A series of delicate peace deals were brokered, with the Persians promising that they would never again attack the Byzantine Empire during Justinian's lifetime. Justinian, on the other hand, was forced to pay an annual tribute to the Persians. While the attention of Justinian and his generals was focused on the Sassanid Empire, back in Italy, things had become very precarious.

War in Italy

In 541, the Ostrogoths began making real progress toward their goal of recapturing the land that Justinian's forces had claimed from them. The resulting war lasted from 541 until 554. The Ostrogoths began by conquering the most important cities and towns in the south of the country and then moved north until they controlled most of Italy. Again, Belisarius, the most illustrious of Justinian's military commanders, was sent to tackle the challenge of retaking Italy. After a major success against a large fleet of enemy ships, Belisarius found himself ill-equipped and failing to gain any ground against the better-equipped Ostrogoths. Both sides would make important gains only to suffer heavy losses soon after; Rome itself was captured and recaptured by each side multiple times. Belisarius was removed from command in 548, which was when General Narses took charge.

In 552, in a decisive move, Justinian sent over thirty thousand men to Italy, where they attacked the Ostrogothic capital, Ravenna, under the command of General Narses. It took a matter of weeks to overthrow Ostrogothic King Totila. Soon afterward, the Battle of Mons Lactarius took place. This was to be the definitive moment, and the Ostrogoths were defeated, paving the way for Justinian's forces to reclaim Italy. Pockets of resistance from Ostrogothic strongholds had to be eliminated, and the threat of invasion from bordering territories had to be pushed back, so large garrisons of soldiers were established for the purposes of defense. The number of deaths amongst the Ostrogothic population as a result of the war was estimated by the writer Procopius at fifteen million. Italy was now a part of the Eastern Roman Empire—Justinian had succeeded in reclaiming the original home of the Roman Empire. The Ostrogoths who survived this period were absorbed into the Lombards, a Germanic people who would later set up a kingdom in Italy in 568 and rule much of the peninsula until 774.

Expansion, Expansion, Expansion

Justinian was absolutely set on expanding his empire and took every opportunity to surge forward into other territories. Justinian's armies entered Hispania, again by offering assistance during a period of political upheaval, and captured a swath of land in the south of the country, founding Spania in 552. He also ensured that his own borders were defended with absolute rigidity; threats from incursions in the Balkan territories were countered with force and diplomacy. Justinian was careful not to focus so intently on expanding the empire that he might neglect defending his territory.

At its peak, Justinian's territory, which came to be known as the Byzantine Empire, spread right around the Mediterranean.

Chapter 6 – Religion

After the Eastern Roman Empire, or Byzantine Empire, was taken over by Constantine I in the year 312, Christianity became the official religion. Constantine I had experienced a religious conversion and had embraced Christianity, making it his mission to found a great city that would unite the people and act as a center of Christianity. This city was Constantinople, which was founded in 330 on the site of the ancient city Byzantium, and it was named after the great leader. Constantinople became the focal point of Christianity in the East.

Justinian's Religious Role

As the emperor of the Eastern Roman Empire, where church and state where inextricably linked, Justinian was viewed as a religious figure as well as a political leader. The religious aspect of his role was one he fully embraced, and he led the empire through a period of religious reform. Justinian was a passionate advocate of Christian Orthodoxy and set about enshrining this in law, opposing other forms of Christianity and eliminating any traces of paganism.

Justinian and Theodora - Religious Conflict

Justinian and Theodora, while considered to be one of the great power couples of world history, disagreed when it came to issues of religious doctrine. The particular aspect of Christian doctrine that divided them was one that divided the Christian world at the time.

This was the conflict between Monophysitism and Chalcedonian Orthodox doctrine. Previous emperors had been tolerant of the different Christian sects and their beliefs, and this had caused tension between them and the leaders in Rome. Justinian sought to change this; he wanted closer ties with Rome, and this meant rejecting Monophysitism.

Monophysitism was defined by the belief that Jesus Christ was of one divine nature. This viewpoint had been declared heretical by the Council of Chalcedon in 451, which asserted that Jesus Christ had both human and divine natures. This belief in the dual nature of Christ became known as dyophysitism. Monophysitism was a doctrine that was widely accepted in Syria and Egypt and one which Theodora was a passionate believer in, most likely as a result of her travels in Egypt, where she had spent time with a religious community.

Justinian was opposed to Monophysitism, both for reasons of religious belief and for political reasons, as the Monophysites resented the rule of Constantinople. However, he did not want to alienate either his wife or the Eastern provinces where Monophysitism thrived. He was also aware that permitting Monophysitism in the empire would inevitably alienate him from Rome. And so, Justinian aimed to reach a compromise that would be accepted by both opposing groups. He tried to manipulate important church figures and even held Pope Vigilius—considered to be the first Byzantine pope—in Constantinople against his will in an attempt to gain concessions from him, even going so far as to compel religious leaders to produce writings permitting Monophysitism.

However, Justinian's attempts to force the issue did not work. Rather, they backfired, with the Council of Constantinople meeting to reject the bogus writings and reassert the Chalcedonian doctrine in 553. Instead of reaching a compromise or obtaining some kind of religious tolerance between the two opposing doctrinal beliefs, Justinian had only enraged both sides. The Monophysites felt that they were still oppressed, while the religious leaders were angry at having had their doctrinal beliefs undermined. Justinian's treatment of the pope earned him condemnation from Rome, and the resulting conflict led to an even greater religious schism.

Theodora does not appear to have ever given up her belief in Monophysitism. She actively undermined Justinian's efforts to promote the Chalcedonian doctrine, going so far as to found a monastery that offered sanctuary for Monophysite leaders and inviting those under threat to have safe shelter in her palace in Constantinople. She put in place Monophysite patriarchs in positions of religious power, often outwitting her husband and establishing her choice for a religious leader before Justinian could. As a result, Theodora was blamed for undermining the religious unity of the empire and was accused of heresy.

Interestingly, Justinian himself turned toward Monophysitism as he grew older, offering the same protection that his wife had afforded to religious leaders and becoming more and more interested in the intricacies of religious doctrine toward the end of his life. Historians have often debated whether he had great personal faith, or whether he cleverly used religion as a tool with which to attain and secure power over the populace. Toward the end of his life, when his power was waning, it appears that it was Justinian's own personal faith that occupied him. He is attributed with the quote, "There are two great gifts which God, in His love for man, has granted from on high: the priesthood and the imperial dignity."

Religious Life and Religious Law under Justinian

Justinian's despotic approach to the keeping of the law in his empire was mirrored in the religious sphere. Despite the obstacles he faced in doctrinal matters, his authoritarian approach to imposing his religious doctrine meant that the religious lives of his citizens were tightly controlled. Religious doctrines were enforced by the Justinian Code, and bishops had to carefully follow his lead on doctrine and teachings. Strict legal rules controlled the clergy and religious administration; however, they also afforded protection to monks, allowing them to inherit property and ensuring they received wealth from taxes.

The Hagia Sophia was the most impressive religious monument that was built by Justinian. When it was finished in 537, he is recorded as gazing upon it and exclaiming, "Glory to God who has thought me worthy to finish this work. Solomon, I have outdone you!" The Hagia Sophia comprised many shrines, smaller chapels, and religious art, the most famous of which are the mosaics (many of which depict Justinian and Theodora). Other churches, monasteries, and religious monuments were also completed during Justinian's rule, resulting in a flourishing of religious art and church-building during this time.

Religious Persecution

Religious persecution of those who followed pagan beliefs was absolute. Even citizens of high status were punished for following any practice or belief considered to be pagan. Pagan practices were not permitted either in public or in private. Justinian ordered the destruction of sites where pagan activities took place, such as the worship of Amun and Isis. Bishops were sent as missionaries to convert pagans, most notably John of Ephesus, who traveled in Asia Minor. Justinian also closed the famous Academy at Athens and exiled the pagan teachers there.

While Judaism was not forbidden outright, those of Jewish faith had their civil liberties denied, and Justinian made changes to how the synagogue was managed and what doctrine was supported. When faced with resistance, for example from the Samaritans, Justinian acted swiftly to persecute those who would not convert. This resulted in a violent conflict between the Christians and Samaritans, an ethnoreligious group closely related to the practitioners of Judaism. Manicheans, a major religious group founded by an Iranian prophet, were among the most violently persecuted, and it is recorded that Justinian had a number of Manicheans drowned or burned in his presence.

Justinian did manage to rescind the doctrinal policies made by his predecessors that permitted Monophysitism and had created a wedge between Rome and Constantinople. This enabled a stronger link between the East and the West and earned him credit for restoring the Roman Empire. However, the conflict between the different doctrines still raged within Justinian's empire, and this resulted in the persecution of those who did not agree with Justinian's doctrines. To modern readers, his religious policies might seem extreme, with the empire striking us as a prime example of church and state being linked to the detriment of the citizens. However, the beliefs of the time held that Justinian was a representative of Christ, and so, his religious authority was accepted. The Eastern Roman Empire and the Orthodox Christian Church were inextricably connected; the religious doctrine was enshrined in law, and political decisions were bound up with religious aims. As a result, the Christian Orthodox Church was undoubtedly strengthened and spread exponentially from Eastern Europe, extending across the world. The modern Orthodox Church has two hundred and sixty million baptized members.

Chapter 7 – Life under Justinian

Justinian is best known perhaps for his rewriting of the Roman laws and the impact of his reign on the religious landscape of the empire and beyond. However, he is also recognized for his architectural legacy, his patronage of the arts, and the economic development of the Eastern Roman Empire under his reign. How much of his encouragement for artistic practices and funding of buildings came from genuine interest and how much was an attempt to secure his own dynastic legacy and compete with the patronage of the arts from other important figures can only be guessed.

Architecture

After the Nika riots, Justinian set about reconstructing Constantinople, rebuilding damaged areas bigger and better than they had been before. The Hagia Sophia, designed by Isidore of Miletus and Anthemius of Tralles, is the most famous example and represented a turning point in Byzantine architecture that would influence buildings across the empire and beyond into the future. However, this was just the pinnacle of the wider urban reconstruction that characterized Justinian's reign. The writer Procopius was tasked with the job of recording the architectural achievements of the emperor in a treatise he composed, entitled, *On Buildings*. There were many new churches, including the highly regarded "Church of the Holy Apostles," and a wide range of secular buildings established under the patronage of Justinian I, which were built all across the empire. The architecture was advanced, and so were the decorations inside and outside of the buildings. Artists were employed to create sculptures, paintings, and elaborate mosaics to adorn the most important buildings, and Justinian ensured that no expense was spared.

Built Infrastructure

As well as buildings, important advancements in built infrastructure were made. Extensive fortifications were built to protect the borders of the Eastern Roman Empire, and a complex arched dam was constructed at Dara, an important border settlement, in order to prevent flooding. Constantinople was growing in size, and to ensure a reliable source of water, vast underground cisterns were built. The largest of these is the Basilica Cistern, but hundreds of these cisterns still lie under Istanbul, which was where Constantinople once lay. New bridges were also built to facilitate travel, trade, and military maneuvers. The most impressive of these was the 430-meter-long (almost 1,411 feet) Justinian Bridge, also known as the Sangarius Bridge, which was built to connect Constantinople with the Eastern provinces. Earthquakes frequently caused damage to cities within the Eastern Roman Empire, and Justinian was quick to restore the damages and prevent civil unrest.

The Decorative Arts

Diptychs were one of the art forms that enjoyed the rich patronage of Emperor Justinian. Diptychs were elaborate ivory panels that depicted the emperor and symbols of the empire, such as acanthi, lions, and religious scenes. The production of diptychs was an important tradition that was furthered by Justinian.

Icon painting also thrived under Justinian's rule, which was the painting of religious scenes and symbols using a traditional technique involving pigment in hot wax. Diptychs and icon paintings were often sent to monasteries or dignitaries as gifts from Justinian. As a result, a large number of important artworks could be found spread across the Byzantine Empire.

Literature

As well as the decorative arts and crafts, Justinian I was an avid patron of literature, especially the recording of history. A number of important writers emerged, the most notable of these being the historian Procopius. Poetry also thrived under Emperor Justinian. The poet and historian Agathias composed many epigrams, poems, and essays, as well as historical works.

One of the more favored poets supported by Justinian was Paul the Silentiary, who composed the following poem about Empress Theodora:

Theodora by Paul the Silentiary

> Scarcely has the pencil
>
> Portrayed the girl's eyes,
>
> But not at all of her hair nor
>
> The supreme lustre of her skin.
>
> If any can paint the sheen of the sun,
>
> He will paint the sheen of Theodora.

Agriculture

The main source of income in Justinian's empire was generated through agriculture. Under Justinian, trade thrived, and produce was sold widely within and outside the empire. Wheat from the Byzantine Empire was traded as far away as India. The Byzantine trade even reached England, where valuable tin was obtained. To facilitate agricultural trade, Justinian built large granaries to store produce at strategic points along trade routes.

Silk

At the time of Justinian's reign, silk production was introduced to the empire. Silk had been an important traded item throughout Eastern Europe for centuries. Raw silk was brought into the empire from China and woven into high-quality silk, which was then transported for trade. When silkworm eggs were secretly smuggled into Constantinople by monks, a thriving silk tradition began, and the Byzantine Empire would go on to become famous for its silk production.

Wealth and Administration

The Eastern Roman Empire was wealthy when Justinian became emperor. The imperial treasury was healthy, but there was still a lot of corruption and inefficiency in the collection of taxes. Tax reforms enabled Justinian to reduce corruption and collect more taxes at a greater speed. This coincided with a campaign of simplifying the complicated—and sometimes contradictory—administrative procedures. In the same way that Justinian sought to rewrite and reform the law so that it was easier to understand and enforce, he also made the administrative practices more streamlined, getting rid of unnecessary officials and redistributing the balance of power across the provinces. As a result, Justinian was able to increase the revenue of the empire and invest it in military campaigns, infrastructure, and building projects.

Pestilence, Natural Disaster, and War

Life undoubtedly improved for the people of the Byzantine Empire under Emperor Justinian I; they benefited from greater stability, increased wealth, less corruption, and simpler laws and administrative procedures. Education was allowed to flourish, and Justinian's emphasis on trade meant that agriculture and mining also thrived, resulting in higher incomes for most citizens. However, there were a number of serious obstacles and setbacks to contend with that undermined the beneficial changes that Justinian had implemented.

The wars in Italy and Persia were a serious drain on the empire's finances, while the presence of opportunistic invaders near the borders was a constant threat. Religious persecution made life dangerous for those who did not conform to Justinian's religious laws, and it was fairly common for conflicts to erupt between different sects and ethnoreligious groups.

A fast-spreading epidemic of bubonic plague, known as the Plague of Justinian, ravaged the Eastern Roman Empire between 540 and 543, damaging the economy and devastating the population; millions died as a result. Justinian himself suffered from the plague during this outbreak, but he survived and recovered, which was out of the norm for the time period. At its peak, the Plague of Justinian was responsible for five thousand deaths every day in Constantinople alone at the height of the disaster. This made it impossible for bodies to be disposed of properly, and the plague spread faster as a result. Mass graves were dug, towers were filled and sealed with bodies, and mass burials at sea resulted in corpses washing up, again spreading the disease.

Perhaps the most mysterious of obstacles to everyday life in the time of Justinian was the unexplained pollution of the air that occurred; dust and fumes blocked out the heat of the sun and caused famine while the people fell sick. This bizarre occurrence is likely to have been the result of the passing of a comet, the gases released by a number of volcanoes, or a combination of the two. This was followed by a major earthquake in 551, which caused a devastating tsunami and claimed the lives of around thirty thousand people.

It is understandable that the people of the time believed that they were being punished by God. In fact, this period was a time of great superstition and petitioning to God for mercy. Most people believed that the plague was the manifestation of evil and sought exorcisms for those who suffered from it. With disease killing large swaths of the population, natural disasters occurring, and strange things happening to the climate as the very atmosphere altered and the sun appeared to fade, it must have been a time of high anxiety for the people of the Byzantine Empire and beyond.

Chapter 8 – The Decline of Justinian

In 548, Theodora, the beloved wife of Justinian and the empress of the Eastern Roman Empire, passed away, having suffered from an illness that historians now believe to have been cancer. This came as a severe loss to the emperor, who lost not only his wife but his closest and most trusted advisor; Theodora had reigned beside Justinian, almost as an equal rather than just a figurehead. Historical sources tell us that Justinian was visibly moved at her funeral, weeping openly.

The loss of Theodora is seen as a turning point in the life of Justinian, even though he survived her by many years. His attention turned away from the practical details of ruling the empire, and he instead focused his energy on matters of theology. He kept his promises to Theodora that he would continue to protect the Monophysite communities that had always enjoyed her patronage and protection. In later life, his own beliefs were beginning to increasingly turn to reflect those of the Monophysites.

As Justinian was turning away from political matters and becoming more occupied by spiritual ones, the Byzantine Empire was suddenly faced with a number of disasters in a short space of time. A major revolt of the Samaritans took place in 556; this ignited religious tensions, and the military was under pressure to put down the revolt and restore order. Less than a year later, another major earthquake caused serious damage in Constantinople, including the famous dome of the Hagia Sophia. This coincided with a return of the plague, causing widespread panic.

In the year 559, the Eastern Roman Empire suffered a major invasion by the Kutrigars and the Huns. These troops crossed the frozen Danube, split up, and attacked the northern border. The main army reached Constantinople and had to be routed by the famous general Belisarius, who was called out of retirement by Justinian, and a hastily assembled army of veterans and paid soldiers. Justinian was able to negotiate to secure his border in return for giving the invading forces safe passage back across the Danube. However, once they had crossed back to apparent safety, Justinian had secretly arranged an attack by the Kutrigars' rivals, the Utigars, which rid the empire of the immediate threat that they posed. However, the defenses in the Balkans were failing, and attacks became more common.

The attack on Constantinople also had a damaging effect on morale in the city, and combined with food shortages, it led to civil unrest. Violence and looting flared up regularly, Justinian was in debt and had been forced to borrow capital, and the business people in the city were disgruntled. In 562, there was a conspiracy to overthrow Justinian. Several business leaders planned to depose Justinian, and although they did not succeed, the attempt gives historians insight into the turning tide of his popularity. All of this meant that when Justinian passed away from natural causes at the age of 83 on November 14th, 565, rather than mourning him, there was a sense of relief and, in some areas, actual jubilation.

Justinian had always relied on the expertise of expert advisors, and in the later years of his life, he was assisted by his nephew, Justin, who was married to his niece, Sophia. His decline from his once-powerful position had been gradual, and he had been very wary of naming a successor, although Justin appeared to be the ideal candidate. Having no children to inherit his role, any named successor would have posed a threat to his continued reign. The story of Justinian's death was carefully constructed by the powerful people around him to ensure that there could be no doubt as to who should succeed him. As such, Justinian's death was witnessed by one member of the court, a man called Callinichus. He announced that Justinian had named his nephew as his chosen successor, and the waiting Justin was immediately crowned as the new emperor. Vast crowds of citizens assembled to watch the funeral procession of Justinian, and his body was interred in the Church of the Holy Apostles, where it lay in peace until 1204, which was when his mausoleum was looted and destroyed by the Crusaders.

Justin II

Justin II was accepted as the new emperor of the Eastern Roman Empire; he had a family connection to Justinian, had some experience of working with him, and enjoyed the support of the head of the Excubitors, Tiberius. Justin II quickly set to work righting some of the problems in the empire as he saw them. He paid off the debt of his predecessor, proclaimed a policy of religious tolerance, and made sure that he was on the right side of the aristocracy. This left him with empty coffers and lots of people to please, and so, Justin stopped the payments of tributes that had been crucial in maintaining peace with neighboring territories.

As a result of the weakened state of the Byzantine Empire and the cessation of tribute payments, Justin II's rule was marked by wars, most notably with the Sassanid Empire. Military defeat followed military defeat, and with the Byzantine Empire under threat on all sides, Justin's once-determined sense of invincibility deserted him, and he succumbed to mental illness. During increasingly severe bouts of his mental illness, he reportedly behaved like a wild animal, throwing himself from windows and attacking his attendants to the point where rumors went around that he had eaten two of his servants. To keep him placated, Justin was wheeled around while organ music played. In short, he was in no way fit to rule.

The madness of Justin II resulted in his wife Sophia convincing him to adopt Tiberius as his son and later to abdicate. As he passed over control of the empire in 574, Justin is recorded as having made a flowery speech offering advice to his successor that suggests that he was still capable of great lucidity and eloquence.

> I have been dazzled by the splendor of the diadem: be thou wise and modest; remember what you have been, remember what you are. You see around us your slaves, and your children: with the authority, assume the tenderness, of a parent. Love your people like yourself; cultivate the affections, maintain the discipline, of the army; protect the fortunes of the rich, relieve the necessities of the poor.

Tiberius and Sophia went on to rule the Eastern Roman Empire together until the death of Justin II in 578 when Tiberius took full control and officially succeeded him. By the time of Justin II's death, the Eastern Roman Empire had lost most of Italy and was struggling financially and militarily.

The Fall of Byzantium

The Byzantine Empire, as the Eastern Roman Empire became to be known, survived until 1453. This is the year when Ottoman forces attacked Constantinople and the city fell.

Up to that point, the empire had seen off many threats, both internal and external. By the year 700, Islamic forces had taken over vast swaths of territory, much of which had been claimed for the Eastern Roman Empire by Justinian I. Lands in Syria, Egypt, and North Africa, as well as across the Holy Land, were lost.

However, due to its reduced size, the Byzantine Empire was wealthier and easier to control. Rather than fading away, it thrived, and in the 10th and 11th centuries, it enjoyed a golden age of art, culture, and development. The beginning of the Crusades marked the turning point for the Byzantine Empire. This succession of holy wars, in which European forces sought to eradicate Muslims, led to steadily increasing friction between the Byzantine Empire and

Western forces. In 1453, the Ottoman leader Mehmed II stormed Constantinople and symbolically entered the Hagia Sophia—one of the great symbols of the legacy of Justinian. The holy building was to become one of the most well-known mosques in all the world. The Byzantine emperor, Emperor Constantine XI, was killed in the battle, and the era of the Ottoman Empire began.

Chapter 9 – Legacy

It is difficult to trace the legacy of Justinian I and the Byzantine Empire because the cultural impacts have become merged with so many subsequent cultures. By its very nature, the Eastern Roman Empire was both geographically and culturally an overlap of Eastern Europe and Western Europe. It began as an attempt to prolong and revive the Roman Empire, but over the course of its long existence, it transformed into an empire in its own right.

Justinian's personal legacy is inextricably linked with that of the Byzantine Empire. The flourishing of the arts during his reign and his impressive record of developing architecture and infrastructure means that there is much to remind the world of Justinian and his influence long after he was gone. How concerned Justinian was with his own legacy can never truly be known, but there is evidence to suggest that he made efforts to leave his mark on history. His impressive building record helped to ensure that at least some of the buildings he commissioned would exist in the future. Like many great leaders before and since, he frequently commissioned writers and artists to record his achievements and create devotional artwork to honor both himself and his empress, Theodora. Some of the incredibly intricate mosaic work dedicated to Justinian is still revered for its aesthetic beauty and historical importance today.

The Restoration of the Roman Empire

Justinian's driving desire was the *Renovatio Imperii*, or the "Restoration of the Roman Empire." While he did not succeed in entirely restoring the Roman Empire to its prior glory, he did reconquer many of the old territories in the West, and he is often referred to as the "Last Roman Emperor." Justinian's hand in this was as the instigator, the financier, and the high commander; he had little to no actual military experience, and his strategic acumen is unknown. It is clear that he entrusted many of the military campaigns to Belisarius. Both men shared similar views: they did not want war for the sake of war or for the glory of it but rather, or so they claimed, to bring peace. Belisarius is attributed with having said, "The first blessing is peace, as is agreed by all men who have even a small share of reason...The best general, therefore, is that one which is able to bring about peace from war." Justinian's break with tradition in handing over responsibility to those who earned it rather than those who were powerful or wealthy contributed to his military and political success.

For over a thousand years after the fall of Rome, the Byzantine Empire, often calling itself the Roman Empire, continued to build on the legacy of all that the Roman Empire had been. Just as the Roman Empire had been a blend of numerous different cultural influences, so, too, did the Byzantine Empire become a melting pot of cultures and ethnicities. One of the major contributions that Justinian bestowed on the world was his rewriting of the Roman laws, which allowed them to persist for much longer than they otherwise would have. Justinian's legal code has formed the basis for law-making across the Western world, and so, as citizens, we are all impacted every single day by his work.

Religious Legacy

Justinian believed strongly that the Eastern Roman Empire must have one unified faith, and he enforced Christianity as the state religion. He ensured that the state and church were inextricable. In doing so, those considered to be heretics were ruthlessly punished; pagans and Jews were pressed and forbidden to practice or express their beliefs. This had an irreversible impact on the religious makeup of the population.

While the empire under Justinian I struggled with various religious conflicts involving complex ecumenical matters, Justinian himself became a revered religious figure. He is widely known as Saint Justinian the Great. The Orthodox Church that formed in the Eastern Roman Empire became the Eastern Orthodox Church, which is now the second-largest Christian Church and stretches across the modern world. One of the main reasons for this religious legacy is due to the large number of impressive churches Justinian built that often featured artwork devoted to him. Enabling his citizens to worship in these grand buildings earned him the favor of the religious population, and this, in turn, cemented his place as a semi-religious figure in the Orthodox Church.

Constantinople

Constantinople, the capital of Justinian's empire, is one of his most important legacies. While it had been an important city for a long time before he came to power, it was the rebuilding of Constantinople after the Nika riots that led to it becoming one of the most developed and architecturally impressive cities in the world. Constantinople became the center of the Christian world. It was not only the largest city but also the wealthiest, with a strong focus on education and the arts. The importance of the city persisted far beyond the classical period and into the medieval period, despite the changes in regime and religion. The Imperial Library of Constantinople can be thanked for the preservation of many important ancient texts; fortunately, some documents were copied and shared before the destruction of the library in 1204 by the Normans. The influence of Constantinople and its culture has had an untold impact on Eastern and Western European cultures, as well as the world at large.

Cultural Impact

The spread of culture in art and architecture in Constantinople and the wider Eastern Roman Empire can be traced far beyond the boundaries of the empire. Religious buildings in Russia, Arabia, and Egypt all show recognizable influences that must have spread outward from the Byzantine Empire. While Justinian's major architectural legacy has to be the Hagia Sophia, there are buildings, churches, bridges, and aqueducts scattered all across Eastern Europe that exist because of Justinian's passion for building.

In the art world, the works of Byzantine painters went on to have a very strong influence on the style of art we associate with the Renaissance. Many of the most well-known Italian Renaissance artists were inspired by the works of Byzantine artists. In fact, many historians go further than this, citing the influence of advanced scholars and artists who left after the sacking of Constantinople and settled across Europe. Many actually moved to Italy, where their ideas and creative endeavors helped to spark the Renaissance.

Justinian and Theodora have always held the fascination of those who came after them, and this is still true today. While some revere them as important religious figures, modern cultural offerings have also been keen to capture some of their stories. They have appeared in countless works of fiction, movies, and even computer and video games. The love story of Justinian and Theodora has become legendary, and their names appear alongside the great romances of the world such as Romeo and Juliet and Antony and Cleopatra.

The story of how Justinian came from lowly circumstances to rise to the top of one of the world's most culturally important empires, restoring the lost territories of the Roman Empire, and his great romance with the most unlikely of women, who in turn transformed the lives of her female citizens, is one that will continue to intrigue people for ages to come.

Check out another book by Captivating History

References

"Corpus Juris Civilis Law: Created By A Byzantine Emperor And Still Relevant In Courts Over 1,500 Years Later." Ancient-Origins.Net, 2020, https://www.ancient-origins.net/artifacts-ancient-writings/corpus-juris-civilis-0011034.

"Justinian And Theodora | Western Civilization." Courses.Lumenlearning.Com, 2020, https://courses.lumenlearning.com/suny-hccc-worldhistory/chapter/justinian-and-theodora/.

"Justinian I." En.Wikipedia.Org, 2020, https://en.wikipedia.org/wiki/Justinian_I.

"Justinian I | Biography, Accomplishments, & Facts." Encyclopedia Britannica, 2020, https://www.britannica.com/biography/Justinian-I.

"Justinian I | Biography, Accomplishments, & Facts." Encyclopedia Britannica, 2020, https://www.britannica.com/biography/Justinian-I.

"Theodora | Empress, Biography, Accomplishments, & Facts." Encyclopedia Britannica, 2020, https://www.britannica.com/biography/Theodora-Byzantine-empress-died-548.

"Theodora: The Empress From The Brothel." The Guardian, 2020, https://www.theguardian.com/lifeandstyle/2010/jun/10/theodora-empress-from-the-brothel.

Bowersock, Glen Warren. *Studies on the Eastern Roman Empire.* Keip Verl, 1994.

Cartwright, Mark, and Mark Cartwright. "Corpus Juris Civilis." Ancient History Encyclopedia, 2020, https://www.ancient.eu/Corpus_Juris_Civilis/.

Cartwright, Mark, and Mark Cartwright. "Empress Theodora." Ancient History Encyclopedia, 2020, https://www.ancient.eu/Empress_Theodora/.

Croke, Brian. "Justinian Under Justin: Reconfiguring A Reign." Byzantinische Zeitschrift, vol 100, no. 1, 2007. Walter De Gruyter Gmbh, doi:10.1515/byzs.2007.13.

Lightfoot, Chris S, and David H French. *The Eastern Frontier of the Roman Empire.* B.A.R, 1989.

Meyendorff, John. "Justinian, The Empire and The Church." Dumbarton Oaks Papers, vol 22, 1968, p. 43. JSTOR, doi:10.2307/1291275.

Procopius. *The Secret History.* Neeland Media LLC, 2019.

Made in the USA
Columbia, SC
15 October 2021

47237092R00033

JUSTINIAN I

While the name Justinian may not be one that instantly strikes a chord with people, his
and his legacy continue to impact people all over the world to this day. It is very likely
as you read this, you are living your life in accordance with laws that came about a
result of Justinian's rewriting of the old Roman codes. Your religious life may have b
impacted by the religious melting pot of the Byzantine Empire, and you may not e
realize it. Perhaps even some of the characters in the books you read, the movies
watch, and the games you play are actually taken from the lives of real people who live
a very different world than ours, and yet they have captured the imaginations of crea
thinkers throughout the centuries.

We know about the life of Justinian from various sources, and as with all histo
accounts, it is important to remember that a lot of history was written with an agenc
mind. This is very true when it comes to looking at the life of Justinian I. The fam
Byzantine Greek historian Procopius is a major source for modern historians on Justin
While Procopius began by praising Emperor Justinian I and enshrining his n
accomplishments, he later villainizes both Justinian and his wife with lots of dam
indictments of their wickedness. It is worth bearing in mind that we cannot necessarily
either the glowing reports written under the emperor's patronage or the outrageous go
written once that patronage was taken away. The truth undoubtedly lies somewhere ir
middle ground, and it is up to historians to try to establish the truth.

What we can be much surer of are the political achievements of Justinian, his impo
legal work, and the incredible record of the extraordinary buildings that were erected i
name. The artistic offerings of the Byzantine Empire under his reign have prod
artifacts that can attest to the flourishing cultural atmosphere of the time.

About Captivating History

A lot of history books just contain dry facts that
eventually bore the reader. That's why Captivating Hi
was created. Now you can enjoy history books tha
mesmerize you. But be careful though, hours can fl
and before you know it; you're up reading way
bedtime.

Make sure to follow us on Twitter, Facebook and Youtube by searching for Captiv
History.

ISBN 9781647486280

9 781647 486280